What the Lake Knows

Also by Brendan Doyle and published by Ginninderra Press
Glass Bicycles
The Wooden Gate

Brendan Doyle

What the Lake Knows

Dedication

This collection is dedicated to my sons and grandchildren,
and to the memory of Deb Westbury,
friend, poet and mentor.

With gratitude to Michele Fermanis-Winward
for her friendship, encouragement and help with the
manuscript.

What the Lake Knows
ISBN 978 1 76109 450 7
Copyright © text Brendan Doyle 2022
Cover image: Brendan Doyle

First published 2022 by
GINNINDERRA PRESS
PO Box 3461 Port Adelaide 5015
www.ginninderrapress.com.au

Contents

Home	7
Sunrise	8
Bush track, early autumn	9
Intruder	10
Breakfast theatre	11
What the Lake Knows	12
November in Blackheath	13
Virago	14
Waves of cold	15
Two magpies	16
Summer Night	18
Pianissimo	19
Rain music	20
Terra nullius	21
Dispossession	22
After drought	23
School Strike for Climate	24
Early election	25
Fire sale, 2000	26
Grounded	27
Both sides now	28
A Dingo by any other name	29
Speed	31
Memorial	32
Little Bay Adventurer	33
Father's Day, Centennial Park	34
Directions	35
A Nest in the West	36
A Villanelle	38
How to paint a portrait of a bird	39

Omid	41
The Egret	42
Condition Q	43
Snow pigeons, Bhutan	44
Tourterelle	45
Reef Mother	46
Berlin, 1975	47
Cwmdonkin Park	48
Dolphins off Camden Head	49
kintsukuroi	50
Still	51
High plateau	52
The Gift	53
Denfenella	54
Winter Song	55
Transitions	56
The Pinch of Time	57
March-fly	58
Doldrums	59
I hate ticks	60
Theatricals	61
The offering	62
Poem for Rachel	63
Words and Music	64

Home

there's a place I call home
on this enigmatic continent

and it's not in the dry heart
nor the steamy crocodile-friendly north

it's not in a traffic-crazed metropolis
nor wind-tormented extremities

but here on the edge
of a vast eucalypt forest
in the lee of the south-west wind

cosy on this wintry morning
warmed by a real fire
where I'm free to dream
my next poem.

Sunrise

goldfish peeks out from lily pad
noting absence
of kookaburra's hungry eye

currawong swoops up from the gully
in purposeful straight line
frog burps its last comment

as dawn paints
branch by branch
the still eucalypts

I too am still –
part of the landscape
of my silent island

Bush track, early autumn

The air so still and sun-charged
I'm almost afraid to move
lest this beauty be sullied
or turn out not to be real

Walking down the track
into painted light
I'm like a pup
open to discover the next moment
in the shimmer
of morning eucalypts

All is as it should be
all nature here
smiling
or benignly indifferent

I smile too
like a kelpie
running after its master

Intruder

By what right does the magpie
watch me disdainfully as I pass
on my early morning walk?
Prior occupation?

It's true, her lineage in these mountains
is more impressive than mine.
Her ancestors were here
when the first tribes arrived.
But all the same…

No, I prefer the little wrens
and honeyeaters
who ignore me
and go about their chirpy dawn business
without looking at me askance

or the gaudy spinebill
hanging upside down
to suck the last drop of nectar
from the purple salvia

or the rosella who looks down on me
benevolently
as I water my morning crop
of doubt and wonder

Magpie must be hungry
lost interest in me
breakfast time
head cocked to one side
listening for worms.

Breakfast theatre

the spider knows
how to fashion
an enticing ambush
from her tiny body

it hangs ingeniously suspended
from two reeds in the pond
irresistible, bejewelled
in the dawn mist

she knows not to make an entrance
until the careless visitor
just passing through
is caught in a deadly net

so far the trap is empty
the spider may have moved on
to multiply her chances
of an early feed

or else the flies
and other delicacies
have spread the word

like all good actors
everyone seems to know their part
in nature's fierce, intricate play.

What the Lake Knows

Autumn, late afternoon I give in to the desire
to move through lake's water and feel its embrace.
Sun still warm, rays filter through weak tea close to shore,
merest shiver of air riffles the dark blue surface.
I step in, it tingles but with the latent warmth
of two days' sunshine.

I lean into the lake, pull its depth into my arms,
take a few strokes,
western sun still well above the tall eucalypts,
sliding through, barely making a ripple,
turn over into a leisurely backstroke
and look around for other presences.

No one, I like that, follow the line of reeds
admire the hanging swamp that filters rain into the lake
now gazing across wind-raised wavelets
I stroke out into open water
and think of the elders who loved this place
before it was changed forever.

Nearing the end of the big curve
that will take me back I hope to my towel and car keys
my skin now attuned to the water's calming hold
with a breath of relief finally back in the tea shallows
I gingerly touch bottom, wary of sharp sticks
and step out onto a thick welcoming mat of native grass.

November in Blackheath

Blackheath holds onto the cold like a terrier,
shaking weary rhododendrons
with mean squalls from the Grose Valley.

Summer? What summer?
It's nine degrees on the old wooden thermometer
and that's in the bedroom.

Sleeting rain outside now
and we're watching Japanese samurai movies
on a laptop, both heaters blazing.

'Biggest dump of snow ever was in November,'
says the newsagent, a native.
'We've had snow on Christmas Day,' he adds with a wink.

Virago

Like a shark provoked
she rips and tears
at any weakness
of habitat or branch,
rough as steel rakes she claws
at whatever stands above ground.

Now hear this! Now feel this!
she cries in defiance
of our petty constructions,
bowls over bins like tenpins
and hurls them
down the neighbour's driveway.

Still not satisfied
she raises a rebellion at two a.m.
and wakes the hapless sleeper.
Nothing to be done,
just listen and hope
it will blow over –

but please not the huge gum
that leans with menace
above my cringing eaves.

Waves of cold

Waves of cold batter
our little human settlement
of fibro majestics.

From Sublime Point
Katoomba town is a meagre raft
on a sandstone ocean.

Wind stops momentarily,
a ray of sun, then rain –
the mountain's haiku.

Moment to moment
learning to love
the ever-changing.

Hey, is that sleet, in October?
only yesterday we played
tennis in shorts!

Two magpies

locked together on the edge of the road
flapping, squawking.
Are they copulating and got stuck?
I've seen that with dogs.
Is one injured by a car
and the other trying to revive it?
I stand and watch
not knowing what to do.

A neighbour comes by with her dog,
sums up the scene.
'I don't want to go near them, she says,
I've got a thing about feathers.'

Should I call WIRES? It will take too long.
I think about intervening
but don't want to get pecked.
I'll walk on, let them sort it out.

An old man in a bush hat gets into his car,
drives slowly towards the birds with headlights on,
stops just short of them, engine running.
Is he going to drive over them,
put them out of their misery?

He gets out and with a deft movement
grabs the two birds, pulls them apart,
they flap about then fly away
seemingly revived.

I go over to the old man.
'They were fighting,', he says with a wry smile
from under his felt hat,
'Beaks got locked together.'

I thank him humbly.
St Francis of Henderson Road
hops back into his car
and motors away.

Summer Night

I come home late
stand outside in the still, warm air
horizon flickers lightning
trees caught in X-ray flashes
I count the seconds to thunder
that rattles like loose roofing iron
listen for the slow-advancing shoosh of rain.

I leave the curtains open
lightning keeps me awake at first
then merges into doze
as I turn my back
to the fading light-show
and drift into deep
storm-laced slumber.

Pianissimo

Before the sounds
of day's busyness
the Bathurst Bullet
lumbering down the line
and the grind of coal wagons
on their long march to China
there's a soft purr
of wind in the gully
to accompany a distant waterfall

Gum leaves stir
a honeyeater fidgets in the banksias
to the doleful cry
of three black cockatoos
spinebill wings whirr
as she hovers beneath a fuchsia

My subtle dawn orchestra tunes up,
soundtrack for a possible poem.

Rain music

All night long
rain music erases dreams
at dawn birds visit my sitting place
on a banksia branch
chick demands food
from mum's empty beak
tiny spinebill
slick with rain
hovers from flower to red flower
without regrets
five rosellas look down at me
from the guttering
as if to say
Are you all right?
make reassuring sounds and
ignoring the seven a.m.
bad news bulletin
fly off to other duties
leaving rain to play on gum leaves.

Terra nullius

You threw sand in our faces
drove us away from the river
told us we were savages
sold us your strange goods
in exchange for lush pasture
that you despoiled
with your sheep and cattle.

We did not poison the rivers
nor cut down the forest
we showed you the way
across the mountains
how to find the waterholes
and could have been your friends
we the elders, the ancient ones.

Although you took our children away
to your coastal towns
and some of them returned years later
with stories of the sea
and towers of money
it may not be too late
to sit around a campfire together.

Dispossession

Homeless is a hard word.
In The Gully, Katoomba,
the tribes had a home
until the revved-up council
gave it over to petrol-heads
men with egos and money to burn.

Today neat plaques decorate
an empty race track
and no one drinks from the stream
that watered a life-giving place
where children heard the old stories
now silenced
where I walk as an intruder
among memories mostly lost.

My white people never signed
a treaty of dispossession.

After drought

At long long last
the sky was able to weep
tears of grief
tears of love
for the parched earth
scorched buds
too early bloomed

and I in the midst of this
wept for the world
too early given up
to the fires of greed and apathy
and added my tears
to the fear and hope
of our angry children

School Strike for Climate

As Judith Wright said,
the message we should send
from age to youth
is not one of fear and pain
but of giving and loving

So when they wag school
to save what's left
of their burning home
we will go with them
hold them in our arms
be fiercely proud of our children
and send them like seeds
to sow a verdant future for us all.

Early election

Dull serenity
is that what we crave
gross national happiness
or gross private accumulation
shares, or sharing?

By the way, how's my super performing today
should we switch to cash?
I feel negatively geared lately
couldn't we smuggle a few more
visa overstayers into the factory, dear?

I'm voting for tax cuts
it's not time to make a change
Tony's done us proud in Warringah
I don't need an ex union boss
telling me what to do, do you?

Fire sale, 2000

A question not, as some may think
of Shakespeare and show ponies
but more fundamental culinary matters
such as who eats whom, and at what price
here in late industrial suburbs
threatened by longevity
and bored indifference.

People dream their way into tomorrow,
screened off from the institutions of yesterday –
church, family, decency –
consuming tacky sentimentality
on current affairs programs
black or white it's all the same
between the ad breaks.

Don't you sometimes wonder, fit to burst
by what algebraic journey we reached
this end of millennium fire sale
how the disaster corps managed to avert
a show-stopper of smoky nightmares?

Grounded

On the edge of the gritty car park
an old bundle of a man totters and falls,
walking stick and bag in the gutter.
A young man gets to him first
holding him like a limp doll.
I pick up his stick
worn smooth like my own father's.

His face is lumpy and wrinkled
a shiny round patch on his head
like a plug from an operation.
Silly old bugger, he mutters
as a council worker steps up
and quips with a grin,
Who's callin' me a silly bugger?

The three of us stay with him
a few more awkward minutes.
Sure you're okay?
Yeah, I'm all right
and hobbles off with his shopping bag
as we exchange shy smiles.

Both sides now

with apologies to Joni Mitchell

It started with two towers –
we were told
we had to drone-bomb
wedding parties
to teach the turbaned killers a lesson

Taliban tanks
pushed innocent carcasses
into graves of nonentity
and the blowback began

Killing cartoonists
avenges the prophet
we were told
sending stocks plummeting
in the market of souls

Now the Afghan province
we claimed for democracy
has been stolen back from us
by the same turbaned killers
we are told.

A Dingo by any other name

Quiz question: When is a dingo not a dingo?
When it's been killed by a poisoned bait
in a Wild Dog Eradication Program.

I never saw a dingo as a kid in Sydney
but have learnt the white invaders treated them
with intense cruelty that continues to this day
animals brought here three thousand years before Cook
tamed as companion animals by Aborigines and Islanders.

We were staying in a mountain cabin by the Turon River
a place of peace west of Capertee in the spring of 2019
and came to a gate with a sign in big red letters:
1080 WILD DOG POISON LAID ON THIS PROPERTY

In '51 the graziers called on the CSIRO
'We need a disease like the myxo, for the dingo'
In '52 Queensland dropped a million strychnine baits
over 'dingo-infested land'
and to prove the point built a 3000 mile long supposedly
dingo-proof fence.
Tassie tried the new 1080 on rabbits, then in '54 on dingoes.

Bounties were king in the fifties,
authorities paid trappers a quid for pelts in some areas
and three quid in others.
Strangely, the dingoes left the one-pound areas
and moved to the dearer ones
clearly wanting to be trapped at a higher price.

Menzies allowed atomic tests at Maralinga from '53.
Thirty years on an inquiry found
a family of blacks and their camp dingoes
were living in a 'banned area'
and the testing went ahead anyway.

Sometimes the cruelty backfired.
An 85-year-old man was found dead in the bush,
accidentally shot himself while clubbing dingo pups to death
with his rifle butt.

In '71 the first dingoes in fifty years
were seen at Wombeyan Caves, a total of three.
Dingo problem worse than believed, the papers said.

Premier Wran put a ban
on the use of 1080 in national parks
especially the Blue Mountains World Heritage Area.
The ban was reversed a year later by the anti-dingo lobby.

After the shock of Turon
we went to Secret Creek near Lithgow
where they breed the local endangered species
and made friends with two fine tail-wagging examples
of the stocky Blue Mountains dingo.

Speed

Not quite three
Charlie wants to ride with the big boys
pushes his three-wheeler
with pace and gusto to the skate ramps
zooms along the flat bits
watches his big brother
crash and graze his knee
doing a daring turn
admires the spot of blood Jack proudly shows.
It doesn't hurt, he says through pursed lips.

Pa, push me really really higher
Charlie used to say on the park swing
now land speed's the thing
as he whizzes down the path
to see if three turtles
are still in the creek by the tennis courts.

Back to the ramps
where Jack and the big boys have taken over
Charlie looks up at me for a decision
then scoots along the gravel track
stops near the crossing
and insists we watch cars
bounce over the speed bump.

Charlie smiles. That was fun, Pa.
I smile too, only wanting
this moment to pass
as slowly as a falling leaf.

Memorial

Charlie, three
wants to show me
'the water fountain'
under the banksias

I call little Flynn to come too
it's a sculpted rock, a metre tall
in the shape of a banksia seed
water flows down a channel in the stone
the boys ask me to put a cone on top
to 'waterfall it' down the sandstone face

Then I see the plaque
'In memory of seven local women
who died in the Bali bomb attack
fifteen years ago'

But this sunny winter morning
it's two little boys laughing
playing with water
stone and native flowers

I cannot think of a better memorial.

Little Bay Adventurer

Along the rock shelf at low tide
my five-year-old grandson
hops like a mountain goat
over a tumble of boulders

We stop at holes in the sandstone
that harbour lush tide-fed gardens
where tiny creatures hide
behind curtains of algae

We find cuttlefish remains
and scurrying crabs
then Flynn searches the best way
around the next rocky outcrop
proud of his agility

After two hours I try to convince him
that like the rockpool denizens
we too need to find our next meal.
He considers this, then challenges
with a cheeky smile:
Just to the next headland!

Father's Day, Centennial Park

My friend and I arrive early
and the familiar ponds, paperbarks and sandy tracks
take me back to those endless Saturdays
of wandering, catching carp,
playing war in the sandhills
with the kids of other runners
while my father trained with his harrier pals.

My son has booked a mega-bike, he calls it,
a surrey with a sunroof on top.
Like a circus act we four grown-ups
pedal for all we're worth,
one-year-old Zara and brother Flynn
smiling and laughing
in a basket at the front.

Now I'm a father and grandfather,
three generations together
and today I feel my dad
could still be pounding his way
around the perimeter of this venerable place
that's seen its share of athletes, picnics,
romance in the bushes
for a hundred and fifty years
after we drove out the fathers,
grandfathers and sons
who had loved it
for thousands of generations before us.

Directions

Some tracks aren't marked
with neat green signboards
leading you in a committee-approved direction.
Some tracks are not on maps,
featured in guide books
or advertised in Great Weekends Away,
aren't well-formed
according to an engineer's plan
designed on a computer
outsourced to a contractor.

Some tracks don't lead you
up a garden path,
to a monument,
or anywhere at all.
They may be scrubby and dark,
confusing, surprising,
forbidding even,
the ones you need to follow.

A Nest in the West

for Michael and Joy Morgan and i.m. Michael Morgan,
8 November 2021

They had a dream
of a world more perfect
a community of souls
devoted to the good of all.

They met the cruel money-lenders
and so-called leaders
who worshipped only dollars and self
and wanted them to see the light
but most were already blind.

So they sought out instead
the wise, angry birds
who pecked away
at the rotten flesh of the city
revealing the corrupt bones beneath

and for the sake of all
they built a nest
high on a heath
and called it West Hill
where rare birds could rest a while
and contemplate the distant
sad confusion.

For a time they even moved
the mountain to the metropolis
and offered a nest in a high tower
to the city's needy offspring
who happily flew in
to join the nourishing company.

But the mountains called them back
and one day they observed
a falcon fly over a bridge
which they took as a sign
and that place too they called West Hill.

Seventeen years on
West Hill blooms still
in another glorious spring
of the many-birded dream.

A Villanelle

It's easy to write a villanelle,
A form that doesn't tax the brain,
And it couldn't be that hard to sell.

The formula, does this ring a bell?
Five triplets, plus a quatrain.
It's easy to write a villanelle.

The first line – should I Show or Tell?
Is also the sixth. What could be more plain?
And it couldn't be that hard to sell.

The third line, to make it all gel
Acts as a sort of refrain.
It's easy to write a villanelle.

You certainly don't need to rebel
Nor drive yourself insane.
And it couldn't be that hard to sell.

The last four lines, a mere bagatelle.
What idiot said, No pain no gain?
It's easy to write a villanelle
and it couldn't be *that* hard to sell.

How to paint a portrait of a bird

by Jacques Prévert, translated by Brendan Doyle

First paint a cage
with an open door
then paint
something pretty
something simple
something beautiful
something useful
for the bird
then place the canvas against a tree
in a garden
in a wood
or in a forest
hide behind the tree
without speaking
without moving…
Sometimes the bird arrives quickly
but it can also take many years
to make up its mind
Don't get discouraged
wait
wait for years if you have to
the speed or slowness of the bird's arrival
bearing no relation
to the success of the painting

When the bird arrives
if it arrives
observe the most profound silence
wait for the bird to enter the cage
and when it has entered
gently close the door with the brush
then
erase all the bars one by one
taking care not to touch any of the bird's feathers
Then do a portrait of the tree
choosing the loveliest of its branches
for the bird
paint also the green foliage and the wind's coolness
dust in sunbeams
and the noise of insects in the grass in the heat of summer
and then wait for the bird to decide to sing
If the bird doesn't sing
it's a bad sign
a sign that the painting is bad
but if it sings it's a good sign
a sign that you can sign it
So you gently pluck
a feather from the bird
and write your name in a corner of the painting.

Omid

    means hope in Persian
        his father named him
            he brought hope and excitement
                to his small family

he was a sweet child who loved animals
    he built a shelter for his pets
        who were like close friends

Omid was friendly, witty and strong
    a lifeguard who saved two children from drowning
        who still visit his family in Iran

he was full of life
    impossible not to laugh
        when he was around

all his goodbyes were followed by
    Chakeretam, Nokaretam, a Persian saying:
        you can always count on me for everything

they were counting on him
    for sweet coming moments
        enduring hardships for a better future

What happened to Omid's hope?
    Who made life so bitter for him?

Omid Masoumali was a recognised refugee who was living in 'offshore detention' on Nauru with his wife, with no hope of ever being allowed to live in Australia because he had come to Australia by boat. In ultimate despair, he set fire to himself during a visit to Nauru by UN officials on 27 April 2016. He died in a Brisbane hospital two days later. His funeral was held in Iran on 20 May. This poem is based on a statement from his family.

The Egret

I look at my photograph of Hamed
who left all he'd known
for a better life.
We gave him a prison, then death.
His vigil is tonight.

I turn and there it is, an egret
fishing for tadpoles from my pond
the whiteness of snow
treading delicately as a ballerina.
I feel blessed by this messenger.

Finally she leaves
lifts gracefully out of the reeds
hovers for a moment into the wind
and sails off into the valley.

In Egypt she was the creator of light
this egret, the young man's spirit
a thousand times brighter
than the candles
we will light this evening.

Now she is free to roam the land
where he hoped one day
to belong

Hamed Shamshiripour, aged thirty-one, imprisoned on Manus Island PNG for four years, was found dead, hanging in a tree in August 2017 outside an Australian-run refugee prison in East Lorengau.

Condition Q

A law graduate from Afghanistan
paints houses in the western suburbs
and sends money to his mother far away

I was a troublemaker
he says with a glint,
because of me my family had to keep moving

I made the boat journey
then six years behind wire
from Curtin to Villawood

He smiles through downcast eyes,
nods to a man who has helped him.
'You have a beautiful heart'

Shows me his driver's licence
a silent bureaucrat marked with a Q
which stops him getting credit

or buying a SIM for his phone
to call the family he hasn't seen for nine years
and may never see again.

Snow pigeons, Bhutan

Our picnic interrupted by sleet
we pack up and walk on
to Kila Gompa, a nunnery
perched on a sheer rock face
at thirty-four hundred metres.

Hearts thumping, we climb a steep track
through rhododendron, spruce and blue pine,
sparing tiny alpine flowers at our feet.
Under steady snowflakes
we arrive at the gompa,
take shelter under eaves.
Ugyen and Kencho prepare our warm lunch on stone steps:
spinach soup, red rice, turnips, potatoes and river fish.

A sudden whirr of wings
and a flock of snow pigeons
circles above and below us.
Our hearts soar too
at this flight of joy
for autumn's first white blessing.

Tourterelle

In the plane to Paris
I watch the commemoration
of the latest terror attack on French soil.
After the rollcall of the victims
and the speeches
the gathered crowd bursts into the Marseillaise –
'Let the blood of an inferior race
water our fields.'

*

Disgorged at dawn from two A380s
we make a ragged queue
heading for the *Police des frontières.*
Avoid crowds, we were warned
and here I am trapped in a narrow corridor
and not a gendarme in sight –
probably still having their coffee and *gauloise.*

*

In the train from the airport I'm advised
to check under my seat.
I do, of course, but feel no safer
and don't breathe out until I'm far away
in the village of Saint-Chels
on a ridge overlooking pastures and solid farmhouses,
sitting outside with friends.

As morning sun lights chestnut leaves
instead of the news
we listen to the comforting song
of a turtledove.

Reef Mother

In the moonlight
a small crowd gathers.
She comes in on the high tide
after midnight,
pulls her ponderous weight
up the crushed coral beach.

We stand in awe
of her long, patient labour.
A child says she saw
a hundred eggs
buried with beak and flippers.

At sunrise we are mute witnesses
to the ageless sacrament.
Her work complete, she turns away
from her anonymous young,
drags herself seaward,
stopping now and then to rest.

We watch transfixed
at her cumbersome beauty
as she slides weightless at last
back into the ocean,
gliding over the reef
leaving her progeny to nature
and us in a state of grace.

Berlin, 1975

Checkpoint Charlie
and they cross between two worlds
in the Renault 4
le jeune couple australien
two fair innocents with an F on the bumper
a tent and inflatable canoe.

Checked for drugs or dollars
waved through with their excitement intact
as if they'd pulled off a plot worthy of Schindler
gladly parting with deutschmarks
to be allowed to see the other side of the cold war.

Parting the magic curtain
they glimpse the tawdry dullness of communism
the lack of capital in the capital
greeted with curious stares in an austere coffee house.
Finally in the GDR, Erfurt, Leipzig, Karl-Marx-Stadt
they are offered precious notes
for the jeans they don't have.

Then Poland and Auschwitz,
a theme park museum of mass murder
tidied up in the name of conscience.
Can't breathe again until they're floating on a Masurian lake
looking back to the shore
where happy east bloc campers
relax by their cheap tents
on the party-sponsored workers' week off.

Cwmdonkin Park

In the dawn mist
a gangly young whippet
tears after a squirrel
in the green hilly park
where the boy Dylan Thomas
chased fantasies and ghosts
and played practical jokes
on the crotchety park keeper.

Drizzle-drops catch
in the petals
of fading white camellias
as the squirrel easily evades
the over-eager pup
distracted by all that's alive.

Dolphins off Camden Head

I looked down from the ochre headland
at you, whirling like a girl
on the empty beach.

The great gulf of air between us
was pain and exhilaration
like the hungry sea eagle circling.

In the dark swell below
a black fin, then three more.
I ran down the headland yelling
Dolphins! Dolphins!

Leaping clear of a wave,
they moved on down the coast,
your distant heart and mine
following in their wake.

kintsukuroi*

Bad things can happen
in the kitchen
she broke a plate I loved
for its rustic portrayal
of a provincial farm scene
which I'd bought in France
thirty years before

I glared with sullen wrath
'It was an accident!'
the farmer's right leg severed
his orchard fractured in three
she wouldn't look at me
without another word
took it away
for a week or two
and repaired it
with great care and patience

Now the jaunty farmer still follows
his handsome draught-horse
past thatched farmhouse
and although we too have split
I treasure that plate
more beautiful
for having been broken.

kintsukuroi: Japanese art of repairing broken ceramics

Still

in memory of Marion Doyle 1951–2014

My niece sends me pictures
of her mother, my sister Marion
a series of snapshots
of her life and mine
intertwined
like wild roses
climbing a broken wall.

Holding babes and pups in her arms
she looks out at me.
Orphaned by time
I yearn for the love
in her shy smile
that is slowly
fading to sepia.

High plateau

i.m. Deb Westbury 1954–2018

The day we met
you showed me the power of naming things
birds, flowers, feelings
whereas I had tried
to find the essence
and missed the detail

At the end of the workshop
I gave you a lift to Central
for your train to Katoomba
and yearned for the high places
that lived in you

So began a friendship in verse
shared on these high plateaus
finding names for what matters
an eastern spinebill in the snow
as it hung in the air
sucking nectar from a fuchsia

or when a hundred galahs
soar and swirl for joy
riding warm waves of air
high above the Grose

I sit in silence at dawn
on the edge of the valley
and look to meet you
in the gentle light coming over the ridge.

The Gift

in memory of Deb Westbury

A sombre mist hung over us
in our padded armchairs
while she waited for death
on her terms
her loving spirit still strong
in the decay of flesh
her passion for poetry
something to cling to
to take us beyond.

Like an alchemist
she changed her loss
and suffering
into art
tears watered the garden
of her poetry
sustenance for the desert days
that she gladly gave
to anyone who would
listen and receive.

Denfenella

in memory of Blue Mountains poet Denis Kevans, 1939–2005

When craven politicians are forgotten
and their names covered over with slime
and their tasteful caskets are rotten
Oh poet, it will still be your time.

When the ocean is lapping round Penrith
and horses and buggies are back
the pilgrimage to Denfenella
will become a well-worn mountain track.

Your heart was as big as your laughter
your mind was as big as the plain
your dreams were the dreams of the people –
Will one such come this way again?

As I gaze at galah and rosella
under deep blue mountain heavens
I like to think Denfenella
was named after you, Denis Kevans.

Winter Song

Not skating away on a river like Joni
nor in a deep and dark December
but scrabbling for kindling in mid-July
here on the edge of the Grose

I recall the last time it snowed
before they changed the climate
I'll just watch tadpoles and wait
for the eventual croak

My son recommends reverse cycle
but I can't turn the clock back
over seventy years
with its bevy of regrets

A south-west gale scrambles thoughts
with no letup
tests my resilience
as I hope for another spring

I want coddling and cuddling
but will settle for a flurry of snow
settling on daphnes
blooming for the first time

and to sing in Rachel's choir
on a frigid Tuesday night –
a poultice of healing music
here in the winter of my life.

Transitions

the lake
shrouded
in cloud

waterbirds
posed
on a grey canvas

no horizon
just grey water
melding into fog

death
may be like this

to walk slowly
into dense
endless mist

without hope
without fear

The Pinch of Time

Get on ya bike, someone said.
What if the bike's old and rusty
and missing a gear or two?
Such is the life of a senior,
always trying to catch up with something.

Too many distractions, there's the rub
and so little time left.
Count the years on a couple of hands
or one
and make each day worthwhile
not forgetting to defrost the fridge occasionally.

Lighten up the darker corners,
find the child within
that you scarcely remember
and make friends with him.

The writing on the wall
may need some deciphering,
a rosetta stone of memories,
invitations to be yourself
and meet yourself again
in multiple exposures
every last day.

March-fly

At the end of a sandy track in a wild valley
he's built a wooden house
his Japanese temple
where he talks to the finches at sunrise
and has guests stay overnight

Fit as a Stradivarius at seventy
(but takes pills for blood pressure)
he's on good terms with his ex
and has great sex once a week
with a younger woman who lives nearby

Passionate about rocks, he's written a book
that we looked over together
then strolled down to his dam
strewn with yellow water lilies.
I plunged right in, not afraid of the cold,
looking back at him, uncircumcised
wading on the edge

Then, sun-dried and dozy
I went for a siesta
in the elegant guest room
with shutters open to nature
but a march-fly kept biting my ankle.

Doldrums

Sometimes the evening ends
in sombre squalls
then dead calm falls
upon the choppy waters
and like a sailor becalmed
I wait on a sea of lead
for a new wind
to lift my sails
dreaming of Atlantic gales
and the voyage
to my Aran Islands.

I hate ticks

Byron Bay
nineteen seventy-three
meditating under a tea-tree
a dozen ticks in my long locks
the chick with me says yuck
tries to flick them off with a sock
they fall down her frock
I take stock
flick the frock over her head
to trick the ticks
too late, they've gone bush
she screams
and knocks me for six

we go to see the doc
the chick is in shock
I'll have them out in a tick he says
just a little prick
with the numbstick
she won't feel a thing
we wait for it to kick in
tick tock
soon little legs stick out
quick tweeze
gotcha says the doc
the only fix for ticks
she smiles
and I give her a squeeze

geez I hate ticks

Theatricals

Don't look bored
as you tread the boards.
Act the part
even if a good script is lacking.
When the plot gets too thick, or thin,
demand a rewrite.

When in doubt, improvise.
When not in doubt, admit nothing.
It may be just a stage you're going through.
Beware of splinters.

Your role may be discovered backstage.
Don't wait for roses in the dressing room
or a ladder to reach the lights.
Be patient.
The Globe wasn't built in a day.

Every act is important,
even failure to act,
even the final act.

Meanwhile, play all the parts.

The offering

Pulling me up on the leash
Jasper delicately vomits up
a whole chicken neck
in front of someone's rubbish bins.
I lead him away,
leaving the little yellow mess
–which he may be tempted to enjoy again –
but think better of it
as a fellow citizen,
retrace my steps and pick up the chicken neck
but not the accompanying yellow liquid
in a doggy poo bag
which I deposit in said neighbour's red bin
whence it will be transported to landfill
at Blaxland I believe.

A little further on he stops again,
this time to drop on a nice piece of lawn
at the foot of a letter box
the digested remains
of last night's dry biscuits
– Ah, that feels better! –
wags his tail
and looks up at me:
Well, what are we waiting for now?

Poem for Rachel

She brings the gift of music,
she knows a thing or two
about rhythm, composition,
tone and harmony
but most of all
the sharing of love
and the bright chorus of community.

We arrive a little stooped
from the weight of the everyday,
breathe out our troubles,
each in-breath
a meditation on beauty,
native bees humming round our queen
in the super-organism
we call our choir.

Words and Music

Chopin at sunrise
plays on me
sends me notes
from a loving friend

To craft a poem
as he did music
composing harmony
of form and feeling

But words betray
pulled this way and that
evasive as eels
in currents of thought

I sometimes feel
like a dilettante
translating an ancient Bhutanese
yak-herding song.

www.ingramcontent.com/pod-product-compliance
Lightning Source LLC
Chambersburg PA
CBHW070337120526
44590CB00017B/2920